A RIDE
TO REMEMBER

In The Alberta Rockies

THELMA JO DOBSON
LILLIAN CATON MAJOR

Order this book online at www.trafford.com
or email orders@trafford.com

Most Trafford titles are also available at major online book retailers.

Printed in the United States of America.

ISBN: 978-1-4269-7075-7 (sc)
ISBN: 978-1-4269-7076-4 (e)

Trafford rev. 06/13/2011

 www.trafford.com

North America & international
toll-free: 1 888 232 4444 (USA & Canada)
phone: 250 383 6864 ♦ fax: 812 355 4082

A Ride To Remember

By

Thelma Jo Dobson
Lillian Caton Major

Photography by Lillian Caton Major
Photo restoration by Jacqueline Price.

Beth and Ray Mustard - Guides to Special Places.

For Our Families

Table of Contents

Introduction

"**H**ere's your horse!"

Tom was leading a saddled horse over to where I stood. He passed the bridle reins to me.

My horse! I was to have my own horse!

"His name is Breezy. He'll be your horse for the whole trip. You can get on, and I'll come around and adjust your stirrups. We're about ready to start."

Before I got into the saddle I talked to Breezy a little and gave him a friendly slap, just to get a bit acquainted. He was a good-looking horse, medium height, all brown, not a white patch anywhere. He held his head high, interested and ready to go.

Soon enough we began to move along a lake shore trail, eleven horses single file. We were on our way! For ten days we would ride a trail through some of the most breathtaking mountain scenery in the Alberta Rockies.

It was July 4, 1947.

1
The PLAN

Albertans know that our Rocky Mountains are a huge attraction. People come from all over the world just to look, or to take part in the multitude of activities that are available. For whatever other reason they come, they almost always want their trip to include stay-overs in Banff and Jasper. When friends or relatives come from far away and we take them to the mountains we have to make sure we don't miss those spots because when they get home the first thing they will be asked is "Did you get to see Banff and Jasper?"

In the spring of 1947 in far-away Ohio, USA, three physician buddies, here just called "the doctors" talked often about the Alberta Rockies. In the doctors' lounge great yarns were told by others who had been there. The three were sportsmen, holding onto their own dream of big game hunting in the Rockies. That dream had been put aside for the previous few years; while their country was at war they had been totally consumed by their work, both at home overseas.

The war was over, cars were again rolling off the assembly lines, on day one after the war's end gas rationing had been lifted. Folks could buy all the gas they wanted and go wherever they wished. The doctors' talk again turned to "getting up to Canada" and the day came when they said "Let's go". One of them had bought a new car, a big deSoto, and he was eager to be at the wheel, heading down the long road to Alberta.

They settled on a mountain trail ride. They had information about outfitters from ads in Sportsmens' magazines, and they decided on outfitter Ray Mustard, of Nordegg, Alberta as their guide. Off went a letter by air mail. Letters written on thin blue paper, placed in blue air mail envelopes with an "air mail" sticker on them went for seven cents. A letter would get to Calgary fairly quickly, then in four or five days it would get to the Nordegg Post Office. It was the best way. The only other way to communicate would have been by making a convoluted plan for Ray to use a radio telephone in either a forestry office or the office of the RCMP. "Yes", Ray wrote back, he would be available in July to take them on a horseback trip over the mountains from Nordegg to Jasper, sightseeing and pre-season scouting for game. Ray had his pack outfit at a camp near Nordegg.

Horseback! None of the three had ever been on a horse more than three or four times, but they had agreed that would be the very best way to fully take advantage of the mountain experience. Plans were finalized. The trip was to take ten days. They would drive from Ohio to the Nordegg camp where Ray would be ready with his outfit to guide them over the mountains all the way to Jasper.

It was a perfect plan, but one last thing had to fall into place, they could not take the time to make it a return trip by horseback to Nordegg to their car, so they asked if they could take a bus or train back to Nordegg.

That would have involved a very arduous train ride taking several days, so they came up with another idea; could they have their car brought to Jasper?

It didn't take long for Ray and his wife Beth to pick up on that. Beth could drive the doctors' car up to Jasper to meet them at the end of their horseback trip! The doctors agreed.

There was one more problem, Beth and Ray would be trailing back over the mountains with three extra horses, empty saddles on their backs. The horses would have to be saddled, there would be no other place to put the saddles, and they would have to be actually led; this was awkward to say the least. Then Beth had an idea. She knew their nephew's girlfriend Lillian Caton liked to ride and she told her about the trip.

"You know Lillian, you could be in one of those saddles, it would be a great holiday for you."

Lillian took about one/hundredth of a second to agree. Beth said she should ask two friends to come along so she asked me, Thelma Jo Van Kleek, (Jo) if I would like to go on a long trail ride in the mountains.

Would I! Do birds fly? What a wonderful opportunity, I said I sure would. The third person she invited was Theresa Dickinson, (Terry).

We were overjoyed. What an opportunity! The three of us would come along with Beth in the doctors' car and meet Ray at Jasper for the ride home over the mountains.

But wait a minute! It would be so expensive, how could we do it? Those guided trips were all-inclusive, "room" and board and horse supplied, as much as $100.00 per day! Very rich for a first-year teacher, a bank teller and a store clerk. We were barely out of our teens, and never expecting to get to go on a trip like that. Not to worry, Lillian said; Ray and Beth were giving us a special deal, $35.00 per day.

That was an amazing deal, but $350.00 was still a lot of money. We still had a few weeks to work though, a little bit saved, and families willing to lend if need be. No fancy riding clothes though, we would have to make do with what we had.

Planning time went fast. There were two ways Beth could bring the doctors' car to Jasper, one would be to go north to Edmonton and then west to Jasper, the other way was to go south to Calgary, west to Banff, then north to Jasper, this last idea might seem a round-about way, but it is the shortest route, because as the highway goes north to Edmonton the mountain range moves off to the west, further and further away. Besides, going the Calgary way would enable us to take in the sights in Banff, as well as Jasper! The win-win way to go!

Ray and Beth planned a schedule so that we would arrive in Jasper at the right time. Seven days after Ray and the doctor's party left Nordegg, Beth drove down to Rocky Mountain House to pick up the three of us. We had been ready for two days! We climbed into the big DeSoto with Beth and headed down the highway, bound for Calgary.

Love those doctors!!

Lillian, Jo and Beth ready to go

2
Calgary And Banff

On The Trans Canada on our way to Banff

In Calgary we first we went shopping for the hats that were a must for the ride. We had a hilarious time choosing our hats. After that Beth thought we should take in a "show", and we chose *The Yearling;* it was showing as a matinee. We then found our way—after getting lost a few times, to aunt Tressa's house, and that's where we stayed the night.

Early next morning we were on the road to Banff, where we were to have a whole day. Strangely enough although it was almost in our back yard, we hadn't been there before. One of the things to do in Banff is climb Turtle Mountain, so we did that first. It's not a big climb, and we girls didn't even go all the way up, but we had a little extra adventure as we took a different way down, got disoriented and lost and had to ask directions. Undaunted and unstoppable we connected with Beth, went for a swim in the hot pool and hiked out to Bow Falls. We stared at the luxurious Canadian Pacific Banff Springs Hotel. We were awestruck by its grandeur. Even knowing it's there, it's a surprise, coming out of the mountains like that. We knew that's where very important people stay when on tour; and we remembered that King George VI and Queen Elizabeth had stayed there when they visited in 1939. To us it was all marvelous, even the pansies on the Administration Building grounds and the shops on Main Street. All the shops! Finally it was time to call it a day, and we went with Beth to her niece's house, where we were invited to stay the night.

Next day we set out on what would become The Icefield Parkway. The first stop was Johnson's Canyon. We hiked right up to the high falls, intimidated by the depth of the canyon and the force of the water.

Beth could have driven non-stop. Her job was simply to get the car to Jasper, but she took time for us to see all the highlights along the way. Our next stop was at Peyto Lake. Beth said "it's a must", and she was right. It was a short steep drive off the road, then on foot for the last stretch to the viewpoint. It was well worth it. We sat there and ate the lunch we brought, feasting our eyes on famous Peyto Lake in its mountain valley. It is particularly beautiful because the glacial silt that drains into it intensifies its turquoise color. Getting the car back down to the main road was steep and dangerous, Beth was going about fifteen miles per hour!

Peyto Lake - Lillian and Jo

Back on the road it was slow going. We found it rough and "washboardy" in places. Beth was a bit worried about the doctors' car getting hit by flying gravel; we didn't meet very many cars though, which was just as well. Most of the time the speed maintained wasn't high enough to make gravel fly anyway. The road had been mapped out and graded by about 1940, but it was not completely paved all the way from Banff to Jasper until about 1960.

Next stop, the Columbia Icefield, it's lowest claws came down almost to the road. We stopped there for a while to stare at the biggest chunk of ice on the continent.

Lillian at the "claw" Columbia Icefield

Lillian and Terry, Athabasca Falls

It turned out to be a very long day, in the late afternoon we stopped in the Sunwapta Falls area for an early supper. One more stop was at Athabasca Falls, another "must see". It was actually frightening to watch the wild torrent boil over the rocks. What if you slipped and fell into that! This raging stream would become northeastern Alberta's mighty Athabasca River.

We got to Jasper late and found a room for the night. Next morning the plan was for us to drive out to the Medicine Lake camp to meet the trail riders, so as soon as we'd had breakfast and gassed up the deSoto we started out, but only a mile or two out of Jasper we met a van, its driver frantically waving. It was Ray and the doctors! We turned around and they followed us back to Jasper for the goodbyes. The doctors were very excited about the trip they had to tell about when they got home. They loaded their gear into the deSoto and left on their long homeward journey, heading first for Banff, one last spot they didn't want to miss! They would be retracing the rough road we had traveled the day before.

Good Bye deSoto! Hello horses! We didn't go back to the camp right then though. Ray and Beth needed to shop for supplies and they had other things to do in Jasper as well, so we found ourselves with most of the day to sight-see.

We decided the way to cover the most ground was to rent bikes. We spent hours pedaling around town and outskirts as far as Jasper Park Lodge—and the Jasper dump! A highlight was watching bears! There were elk everywhere, and we were warned not to go near them, as they could be dangerous. Bears were a different story. They were so habituated to humans they didn't even give us the time of day. They had plenty to eat at the dump, we rode by and saw a dozen or more climbing around on the refuse, busy with their favorite summer pastime, eating. We rode through family groups of them on the road and none of them paid any attention.

Terry and Jo watch bears

Biking at Lac Bouvert

In the afternoon we met Beth and Ray ready to head back to the Medicine Lake camp, our pre-holiday was over, but the best was yet to come! We piled into the back of the van for the ride out to the camp. On the way there was one more "must see". At Maligne Canyon Ray stopped so we could have a look. We were spell-bound, we had never seen anything like it! I looked over the rail at the terrifying deep crack and got curious tinglings in my legs. The canyon is worn very deep by runoff from the Maligne valley and from Maligne Lake, higher up. "It's maybe fifteen stories deep", Ray said. He told us that Maligne Lake was where we were headed the next day.

Maligne Canyon - That Deep Dark Crack!

3

Medicine Lake

The camp at Medicine Lake was high-tech; there were cabins and bunks, but we were too excited to sleep very much. Morning finally came. All we had to do was get up, eat the breakfast prepared and wait for the others to break camp. For me, camp by a lake always meant you go for a morning dip, so while we waited I did that, into that icy cold mountain lake, and that was the fastest morning dip ever. About five seconds and I was really refreshed. That was like no prairie lake!

Strolling around near camp we saw a deer and her fawn, one more bear. Blue jays and squirrels sassed each other.

The wrangler on this trip was Tom. He had stayed out at camp with the horses. Tom had worked for Ray as wrangler on many other trips so they were a good team. A wrangler is an absolute necessity on a pack trip of that size. There is a lot of work to do caring for the horses.

When a wrangler goes looking for a job with a pack trip the first question that will be asked is "Can you throw the diamond hitch?" This complicated arrangement of ropes and knots is what keeps the pack boxes securely attached to the pack saddles on the horses' backs. The most popular way to accomplish this amazing process is described in our Appendix.

One would think it would take a half-day to pack even one horse, but an experienced wrangler accomplishes the diamond hitch in an unbelievably short time. Packing was no problem for Tom, but this is only part of the job.

By the time Tom brought Breezy over to me that first morning he and Ray and Beth had already packed five pack horses, and saddled the six saddle horses. In the wooden pack boxes on the horses' backs was everything that would be needed for shelter and three meals a day for ten days for six hungry people.

For the saddle horses, each horse needs to have the best fitting saddle possible. A wrangler is good at knowing when a saddle fits right. Saddles are all different, since they are all hand made, so it's possible to recognize each one and just remember which saddle is for which horse. Sometimes for that many horses it would be easier to have some identification on the saddle, but Tom and Ray were used to what saddle fit each of Ray's horses. A saddle from the tack room had been chosen for a new horse in Ray's herd, one called "Kitty".

The pack boxes are carefully managed as to what goes in what box and when it's unpacked. The boxes hang on each side of the horse from the pack saddle tree and they must be as even as possible in weight. They could each weigh as much as one-hundred pounds; they are lifted simultaneously by two people, one on each side, and hung on the pack saddle. Across the top of the two packs something else can be placed, for example a rolled up tent.

At last Tom and Ray were satisfied that everything was in order, and we were on our way on this bright summer morning. Lillian always appreciated everything about nature and the outdoors. Nothing went un-noticed; she said "What a beautiful sight, eleven horses single file on the trail".

Medicine Lake Trail

Our trail went along the north-east shore of Medicine Lake. There was Ray and Beth, Lillian,Tom, five pack horses, Terry and me. There were mountains pretty close to us all the way along the lake. In July Medicine Lake is at its highest and longest, about seven miles from end to end. The pace is one set by the pack horses, a brisk no-nonsense walk, (horses with packs don't run), it gets you there, but doesn't create pressure. We saw plenty of wildlife, small animals and birds, and lots of water foul on the edge of the lake. We saw ducks with the most outlandish plumage, dark blue, black-outlined white striping, and spots of white, brown, black and chestnut-red. Beth told us they were Harlequin Ducks. We thought they must have been named that because they looked clownish, like they dressed up in everything they could find, both male and female, although the female was a little less brilliant. Harlequins are mountain ducks, Beth told us, terrain like this is the only place they are found in Alberta.

We were to find out on this trip that Beth and Ray were like encyclopedias of wilderness knowledge.

We followed along the shore for the whole length of the lake, it was so beautiful, peaceful and quiet. Except for bird calls, the thud of hooves and creak of leather were about the only sounds.

We didn't even talk that day, we were just getting used to the idea that we were actually on our way, horseback, bound for Nordegg! On a trail ride that wasn't just for the day, or even for two days, but for a glorious carefree ten days!

Most little girls love horses, and dream that some day they will have their own horse. Reality takes over in most cases, there is no horse, but there we were, three grown-up little girls who could, for the next ten days, imagine that our dream had come true!

I had learned right away that Breezy would be last in the line-up. He could not be convinced to get into place farther ahead. If another horse wanted to wait and be last, Breezy was happy to wait until he or she had given up. He was very patient, and in the end always had his way; he would be last.

After a couple of hours we reached the south end of Medicine Lake and from there on the trail was along the Maligne River. It was more open, there was more room between the mountains and the river. Our trail turned into a narrow road. It was one-lane and rough and we saw that vehicles had used it. We were surprised to find the road there, and Ray explained that during WWII a camp for conscientious objectors was established in that area. A crew of prisoners from a camp right in Maligne Canyon had been put to work on this road from the south end of Medicine Lake to the north end of Maligne Lake. The area was considered remote enough that no one would think of trying to escape.

It was about another twelve miles to Maligne Lake, the trail (road) followed the north shore of the Maligne River all the way. There was spruce bush interspersed with open meadows and patches of willows. We saw our first caribou. Occasionally there were boggy spots. Poles had been laid over soft spots, (corduroy), but the horses chose not to walk on those poles, sidestepping around them, through the soft spot.

We stopped for break time at a little creek that emptied into the river. Ray made a tiny fire on a gravelly spot near the water, filled his "tea bucket" from the creek, and hung it from a stick over the fire. We got our enameled cups from our saddles and in minutes we were sitting on the grassy bank of the stream, enjoying hot tea and, for me at least, a first ever taste of sardine and mustard sandwiches. They were delicious!

Ray said that if we had scraps not to toss anything aside. No people food for the wild animals! Scraps were to be carried to the night camp where they would be burned in a bigger camp fire. Not to worry though, we ate every crumb we were served on the whole trip. The last of the tea went on the fire, plus a few pails of water from the creek. We had a little walk, "to stretch our legs", as Ray put it. Then it was back in the saddle. This mid-day stop was to be the pattern for the whole ten days.

Ray was particular that nothing be left in the wilderness, "Leave as little mark as possible" he said; "make sure no gum or candy wrappers or used band-aids get left behind".

None of us smoked except Tom, and he rarely smoked on the trail. If he did he had a tiny tin can with a tight lid and in there went the butt, and the tin went back in his saddle bag, contents to be disposed of later.

Another couple of hours ride brought us to Maligne Lake. We were almost 2000 feet higher up in the mountains than we had been the day before. That's like going up stairs 200 times, I wondered if the horses noticed.

4

Maligne Lake

At the Maligne Lake camp there were a couple of cabins for tourists and also a ranger station. The ranger was not there but we camped nearby. This was our first real camp, the first time to sleep in our tent, the first time to make our spruce bough beds. Ray and Beth unpacked, set up the tents and started supper, shooing away curious chipmunks.

Back in the bush a little way we cut the armfuls of spruce bows that we would sleep on. On the ground inside our tent we laid them like shingles, starting from the head end, laying them tip ends up, overlapping, next row overlapping the first and so on. Over that went a ground sheet to protect from moisture, on top of that a sleeping bag. Lillian and Theresa had borrowed sleeping bags, I made my own from a thick wool blanket. It works well this way: lay out the blanket lengthwise, fold up one end a few inches for foot space, then pick up one third of the blanket length and drag the folded edge across, laying it along the far single layer edge. For the side near you have some big safety pins to hold together the folded edge on the bottom and the single edge that lies on top. On the opposite side where you are going to crawl in, viola! You have a double layer on top and a single layer on the bottom. I rolled up my jacket for a pillow, all was ready for a good night's sleep.

Meanwhile the horses were attended to, saddles and packs off, they were free to go for their night's graze. Not all of them were completely free, a couple were hobbled. A hobble links their front feet together with a strap so they have to move both at once. That way it's much harder to get very far away. Ray and Tom kept their own horses tethered and moved them during the evening a few times, sometimes they would even get up and move them during the night. Their own horses were the least likely to wander, but needed close by to ride out and bring back those who might.

Back of the lake there were open patches of meadow filled with lots of wild hay. A clear swift stream flowed through on its way to the lake, good water for people and horses.

Camp was soon in order, and surprisingly soon we were enjoying hamburger, bought frozen in Jasper, with beans, onions and cheese, and fruit to finish off with. We had let Beth and Ray know that the dishwashing job every night would be ours. We got that done and went to stroll the lakeshore.

We felt awed by the beauty, and we felt Maligne was more than just another beautiful mountain lake, lying there more than a mile high at 5,479 feet. There was a mystery about it. Maybe it was the inaccessible underground caverns that we were told lie underneath. Maybe it was that deep dark canyon that drains the whole valley, somehow having something to do with Medicine Lake, itself mysteriously disappearing, we had been told, after the summer months. Most of all, why does such a beautiful lake have a name that means wicked? We found out later the folklore is that it was the river's treacherous current where it joins the Athabasca that was indeed "wicked" for early traders to navigate. They began calling it "that wicked river" (*La Riviere Maligne!*) and both lake and pass inherited the name.

Lillian at Maligne Lake

In the late daylight we watched the lake's vibrant turquoise and green reflections soften. It's surrounding high glaciers still gleamed in the late sun. It was quite an extraordinary sight, everything we had been told and more. We were even treated to another special sight, more harlequin ducks!

We weren't the only ones watching the lake. There were a few people nearby, from their conversation we took them to be Americans and we wandered over to chat. (Actually we wondered how on earth they had got there).They were eager to tell us about their adventure. They had come all the way from North Carolina! We were amazed. They were on a very long train ride; they had come all the way to Winnipeg, Manitoba by rail. From there they had tickets on the Grand Trunk Railroad, with berths, to get them all the way to Jasper. They were having a great time, literally living on one train after another.

In Jasper they had found Fred Brewster, of Brewster Tours. He told them he offered a tour by taxi to Medicine Lake, by ferry the length of the lake, and then by touring car (on the primitive road we had been on), the rest of the way to Maligne Lake where he had a few cabins. Wanting to go as far as they could they had signed up.

That still wasn't the extent of their Maligne Lake trip! Boat trips were available for the short jaunt out to Spirit Island in the middle of the lake and they had opted for that as well. Viewed from that tiny island, the whole panorama along with surrounding glaciers was before them, and they said it was like the heart of the whole Maligne Lake experience.

Well, we hadn't been there, weren't going there, didn't even know about it! Sometimes well-researched tourists know more than a local!

We were very proud of "our" lake anyway, and delighted they were enjoying the Alberta Rockies. They asked us all kinds of questions about Alberta, and how one lives through winter!

They felt they were at the absolute pinnacle of wild adventure. When told we girls would be going on over the mountains, on horses, the southern ladies were politely skeptical, doubting that possibility and gently expressing their view that perhaps we were just a little too daring!

Just as we said good night, over the water came the haunting cry of a loon. How Canadian was that?

We went back to our tent and sleep. Next morning we were going to be off early, we wouldn't see our American friends again.

Ray and Tom checked the horses one more time, and moved the tethered ones. These eleven horses each had their own personality and their own story to tell.

5

Meet The Herd

My name is Duke. I'm Ray's horse. I'm big, seventeen hands Ray says. I go ahead of all the rest because I am a leader. Ray is Guide, so of course we go first, but I am the kind of horse that would go first anyway. I don't want any other horse to be ahead of me. Ray and I have been together for a long time. I can't even remember not being Ray's horse. I know what he wants by the way the reins feel on my neck.

We knew something was up when Ray brought all of us in from the grass and penned us up in the corral. He and Tom started checking our feet, trimming hooves, replacing shoes. They looked for scratches, sores or bites we might have. We knew we must be going away. Sure enough, we soon started off with Ray and Tom, the pack horses and three men we hadn't seen before.

We carried them on a long trail, but now Ray has decided we've gone far enough. We've turned around and we're going home. I know the way, I could be the guide! Horses always, *always*, know the way home. We like home, the grass at home is good.

Our whole herd is on this trail. That is our herd and one more. Usually right behind me is Goldie. Her rider is Beth, but Beth hasn't been with us. Goldie just came along with no one in the saddle until we turned around. Beth is here now. Beth and Goldie have been together for a long time as well and are very used to each other. Sometimes if the trail is wide enough Beth and Goldie come up beside me and Beth and Ray talk. Goldie stays back a bit though, she knows she must not try to have her nose ahead of mine, if she does I would just have to go faster, and faster, and this is not a race.

There is Dusty, Tom's horse and he's a "quarter horse", used to working with cattle when he was younger. He would know which animal to go after to "cut out" of the herd. Dusty is very smart. That work was hard and fast, with quick turns, it made his knees hurt when he got older, so he was retired from his job on a ranch. It's an easier life for him now, just being with Tom and going on pack trips. Tom keeps him close, at night he is on a long tether near camp. Tom moves him to more grass a couple of times in the evening, then even gets up in the night sometimes to move the rope to make sure Dusty is still on good grass. He will be grazing for most of the night, like all of us.

We hardly ever lie down; we rest standing on our four legs. You might see us lying down sometimes in a big pasture where there are other horses, but not for long. We're just rolling around, scratching and then we might lie there for a few minutes before we get up. You'll often see us standing "hip shot", that doesn't mean actually "shot", it just means we can loosen one hip joint and let that leg sag. Then we are really relaxed and resting, maybe even dozing.

The three men who were with us when we started have disappeared. I could see they were not that experienced as riders. A horse likes it better if the rider is used to riding. We always know when the rider is not quite sure how to do things. With Ray and me, I always can feel a light rein on my neck, either side, and the pressure of knees on my sides and it's like we are a team and I know exactly what we are going to do.

Those others never yanked the reins or kicked their horses sides or anything like that, mostly it was just that they didn't hold the reins right, and they just didn't look like they were moving with their horse. They leaned a little to the back. They groaned and stretched a lot when we came to the end of a day's trek and that was different. Since they disappeared, on their horses Sam, Kitty and Breezy, are three women, much smaller than the men, the kind you can barely tell are in the saddle, and I can see these ones are good riders.

Terry rides Sam and he just follows along after the pack horses. He's been on a lot of these trips, with different riders. He was very used to different riders when he came here to be part of our herd. He had lived at one of those places where they take people on little trail rides. Those riders are always inexperienced. Their horses can keep grabbing mouthfulls of grass because their riders don't know what to do about it. They flap the reins, yell giddup and kick sides but their horse doesn't pay any attention, none at all, just walks a few steps and then grabs another bite of grass. Ray says those horses get "spoiled". He spotted Sam and brought him home for our herd because he could see Sam was young and strong and would be a good trail horse after a little training, and after we got used to him and he got used to our herd. He was right, Sam stays in his place and does a good job every time, no matter who is riding. He likes Terry, he knows she knows a lot about horses. She lives on a farm, Sam can tell.

Then there's Breezy, he has been in our herd ever since he was a young colt. His mother is not here any more. Jo soon learned that Breezy comes last in the line-up. Last place is his place. Unlike me, (I don't want any horse in front of me), Breezy does not want any horse behind him. Sometimes another horse will want to hang back, not in a hurry to get started after a break, maybe wanting to have a turn at last place, but Breezy will wait, always.

Lillian and Kitty

Lillian rides one who is called Kitty, the new horse. We don't really want Kitty in our herd, we don't know why she isn't in her own herd, we can see she is not comfortable, doesn't know just where she belongs with us, or if she belongs at all. She is restless and keeps wanting a different place, keeps bothering the pack horses. Sometimes she is allowed up front but then she just tries to go ahead—of me! They gave her to Lillian to ride, I guess they think Lillian is right for her, will be able to handle her and will do a bit of training with her. If Kitty doesn't calm down we might nip at her or kick her when we are all close together getting saddled and ready to go, or when we're drinking at a creek.

There are five pack horses in the string. Their names are Sandy, Mae, Girly, Dick and Pete.

I have never been a pack horse myself, in some herds there are horses who do have to double as pack horses sometimes, but I haven't. It's easy to see what it must be like though. Those heavy boxes at their sides just hang there, heavy, dead. I don't think you could ever get rid of them. It would be like they're tied to your back bone. You could get rid of riders; you could buck them off, (not me, I would never do that) but I'm just thinking it would sure be possible to get rid of a rider that way, or you could scrape them off, or roll over and get them off. But those boxes are there for good, until some human lifts them off. You could roll down a mountain and they would still be there, solid, they don't ride, they just hang. If they are pressing a bit too much on one spot—forget it, they stay that way for the day. I've seen pack horses unable to wait until they were unloaded try to roll with the pack still on. They want to scratch their backs and get blood circulating.

Riders move with you, rider and horse look like they belong together. Riders twist this way and that looking around; they get off and on during the day, and when they come around and say "Good boy, (or girl)" and give you a friendly slap on the shoulder it's a good feeling. You could never have the same feeling about a wooden box.

I can see though that it's a very important job that the pack horses do, because for humans life is extremely complicated. Going away from home is huge for them. They bring tents, groundsheets, tarps, bedding, clothes, pots and pans they eat out of, and buckets, axe, stove, shovel, and all the many different things they eat, boxes and boxes and cans and more cans, and there's lots more. Of course some of it is for us, our halters, hobbles and tethers, ropes, extra saddle blankets, salve for sores, tools in case a shoe comes off. Each rider keeps a saddle bag with a little bit of stuff in it tied on behind their saddle. Everything else has to be carried by the pack horses, so they are a very important part of the outfit.

Very important, because I see on the top of one load a fat-looking sack and I know what's in it. It's oats. We got some before we turned back and it looks like we're going to have another treat on the way home. Ray does this for us sometimes if we're away from home for a long time. Grass with a bit of oats now and then is all we need for a good life.

6
Life On The Trail

We broke camp at Maligne Lake site early on our second morning out and headed for Maligne Pass, following Ray on the big white horse! That was our last look at Maligne Lake as the trail turned away from the lake and went straight south for about five miles, then southeast. Before all that though there was the Maligne River to be crossed, just at the north end where it drains Maligne Lake. It's deep and very turbulent as it leaves the lake. There was an old bridge, but it was much too shaky and full of big cracks for the horses to step on. Downstream a few hundred yards there was a ford, not an easy one but better for the horses than the bridge so Ray and Tom took the pack horses and our saddle horses down there and they got across. They used ropes and led Kitty and Sam; Goldie and Breezy followed on their own. We three and Beth walked across the old bridge and waited for them to pick us up on the other side. They got across fine, and came along with our four horses. We didn't even risk getting our feet wet!

We moved out on our second day's trek. Lillian rode up front with Ray and Beth as Kitty didn't want to be behind the pack horses. Terry and I rode after the pack horses, Terry on Sam and me on Breezy, the one who always *wanted* to be last.

For the first couple of hours as we rode south from the lake there was a lot of open area with small brush and willows and we saw game. From Lillian's diary:

"We saw a few deer, and a little cow bird followed us for miles and even tried to ride on the back end of Terry's horse! Later we saw a small herd of caribou, Beth rode toward them, but of course they didn't stick around. They were the first caribou we had ever seen".

We weren't the first to spot them. We soon realized that we were likely never to be the first to see game. When we were in a long line with Ray ahead of course he would be most likely to spot something, but even times when we were stopped for a break or lunch, he would often point out an animal we hadn't noticed, but that he had seen, and often Tom and Beth as well.

Ray carried a rifle, but we never saw it out of the scabbard. No guide would ever come out into the wilderness without a rifle. There was almost zero chance at that time of the year to encounter a marauding bear. Though it's not impossible that there could be an exception, bears like to keep out of the way. Cougars are a different sort, they like surprises, and the surprised one is *you*.

The rifle fits into a scabbard, which hangs from the saddle horn by a leather thong and the case holding the rifle fits back and down under a stirrup. There is, in addition to an attack by an animal, another reason for the rifle, and it's a very somber one. A horse could get a bad sprain, foot injury or even a broken leg. A horse that can't walk must be left behind, but not suffer.

About mid day we had our lunch break, again by a little creek. It had showered there earlier and there was nothing really dry, we wondered how Ray would make a fire, but a huge old white spruce stood nearby, its lower branches hung thick with Old Man's Beard. Ray pulled a handful from the underside of a big branch close to the tree trunk and it lit easily and fired tiny twigs, then bigger and very soon we had the tea bucket boiling. More sardine and mustard sandwiches, along with peanut butter and left-over pancakes rolled up with brown sugar. The six of us made short work of all of it.

Back on the trail, we came into heavier bush with mountains closer on either side. We saw pileated woodpeckers, with their big red heads they were easy to spot. There were lots of chickadees and hairy and downy woodpeckers and blue jays. Squirrels kept chattering.

Maligne Lake is about eighteen miles long including the "Samson Narrows" in the middle. The upper Maligne river flows down from the pass bringing glacier meltwater and entering the main body of the lake just north of the narrows.

We forded several small creeks that crossed our path on their way to the river. We came to the river itself where it still had about five miles to go before it would enter the lake. It was a pretty good size and very fast flowing. To get across we had a choice; there was a bridge. Fords can be difficult, but bridges are not always the answer either, especially old bridges like the one we came to. Though it was old bridge, it looked safe enough and obviously others had been using it as we didn't see marks from fording on the shores, actually the banks were quite steep. We decided on the bridge and started across. Suddenly a horse got one front foot caught in a wide crack. Who else but Kitty? Suddenly noticing that something about the bridge was very scary, Kitty shied a bit, and bingo, her foot was stuck. Lillian swung down from the saddle in a split second to grab her bridle. Tom was there almost instantly as well. Between the two of them they managed to keep Kitty from going completely crazy. Ray found something to pry with and very soon they had her released. She had struggled a bit but fortunately there seemed to be no scrape. If there was an injury that got sore and she started to limp we would be in trouble. That particular spot, just above the hoof, the pastern it's called, can be hard to heal when it gets injured. Although horses are so strong and agile, when it comes to healing a bruise or swelling or scrape, they are babies. As it turned out Kitty was fine.

Next day we did ford the river twice as the trail took us up-river toward the pass and we ran out of trail on one side or the other, but of course the river was getting smaller all the time.

We didn't go too much farther that day, we found a good camp site when we were still about twelve miles from the Pass. Ray wanted to camp before we were too high to find good grass. A mountain meadow is ideal, horses are well nourished by the bunch grass and wild hay that grows thick in those meadows so they are not likely to wander looking for something better.

People on a mountain trail all look for the same kind of place to stop, one with good grass and good water for people and horses. It's not surprising then that people pick the same places and these become regular camp sites. Some of them even have a stone fire ring and logs around to sit on.

At permanent camp sites a little courtesy we were told about was "leave your tent poles". If you have one tent and there are poles for more, don't chop the extras up for firewood. The next party may have more tents. Leave the poles for someone else, and you will find poles left for you at the next camp.

Camp set-up is quick when six people get to work. This was our second day out, we were learning! We pulled the saddles off our horses ourselves and piled them on the ground, where all saddles would be covered with a tarp later. We led our three to the creek for a drink while they waited for Tom, he and Ray were unloading those heavy pack boxes. It was up to Tom to decide who gets hobbled and who gets to go loose or be tethered. Kitty for sure would be hobbled, if not she might just decide to go looking for her old herd.

We dragged our tent to a good spot and found poles, got it set up pretty much ourselves. Two long poles set wide apart across the front of the tent criss-cross at the top to hold the ridgepole. At the back sometimes instead of poles there is a convenient tree to hold the ridgepole. Stakes to hold the rope ties at the sides finish the job. We "gathered" our beds of spruce bows, all the while enticing smells of supper were drifting in the air.

The Main Tent
Packbox table, stove next, wash basin in front.

We had been curious about what we would eat in camp; in other words what kind of meals would it be possible to prepare in camp? We would need a lot! We had only been to camps in parks where there was a store nearby where you could buy something for supper every day. We couldn't think what might be in those pack boxes that would make meals for six for ten days with no shopping.

There was everything!

But first, there was the stove. Some sort of heavy tin box that when opened up had a top to cook on, a little hole at the back fitted with a length of pipe to carry the smoke away, an oven and of course a fire box. This contraption folded up and was carried by one of the pack horses, (one that wouldn't get excited if it rattled a bit.) We were to find out that it was perfectly amazing what could be cooked on it and in it. Beth and Ray were gourmet cooks who could practice their skill even out in the wilderness.

The first pack box opened was the amazing "day box". Like a tiny kitchen it held all the things you reach for every day at home, the basics for baking: flour, baking powder, sugar and salt. There was syrup, jam, peanut butter, spices, coffee, tea, cocoa, and much more, whatever you would have in your own cupboard at home.

Then there was the actual food. We had full hot meals of vegetables and meat every night, and plenty of good sandwiches at noon. Sacks of root vegetables or cases of canned food, milk and butter, canned beef, chicken and salmon went in the bottom of the boxes, bread on top. Lots of bread was needed, we made sandwiches for six every morning. We had fresh meat for a couple of days out of Jasper, then canned meat and chicken and fish, always bacon, and there was a ham for later on.

There was certainly a methodology to arranging the contents of the pack boxes. How to use out of them and keep them balanced for reloading was beyond us, we just enjoyed what came out of them.

After supper we put our dishwashing skills into action, and we leaned how to clean up and pack up the site properly. For tin cans it was bottoms out, flatten the can and pack it all up again.

Beth brought out the cribbage board. We saw that this was a nightly routine for Ray and Beth. On this trip and every trip, every night after chores, out comes the cribbage board. They play one game each night. Equally skilled and competitive, their games could be intense. We did not kibitz! Beth kept a log which would be totaled at the end of the trip. Later sometimes we did join in after the cribbage to play a few games of something more at our level.

The long summer evening was still ahead of us. We went walking and looking, climbing up nearby high places to see what was on the other side. We didn't see any game, that evening. Lillian said "We just don't have the hunters' eyes", but I don't think we were very quiet either. Out of sight of camp we soon got scared and headed back. Just as well, we could very well have turned the wrong way and got lost. After all we had got lost coming down Tunnel Mountain in Banff!

The mountain night was very cool. Lillian and Terry zipped their sleeping bags into one and that was much warmer. I was warm enough in my thick wool blanket.

7

Maligne Pass

Ray had a little silver bell he rang at breakfast time. So elegant! The next morning that breakfast bell rang early, his excellent pancakes and bacon were ready, horses were rounded up, and we were to make an early start for our next day's ride. That was the day we would make it over Maligne Pass. We gathered up our spruce bows and scattered them in the bush, a morning chore; took our tent down and dragged it over to the horses. We helped however we could to clean up from breakfast. Beth finished up and went to help with saddling up. It was very early when we started out, but the July sun was already high.

We girls were somewhat frivolous, one of the things high on our list of needs was to be sun-tanned. To this end we all wore "halter tops" under our shirts and the moment the sun came out, off came the shirts. This was a thing Ray was not able to understand.

The capricious mountain sunshine would be out for a few minutes, then gone and the mountain breeze off the snow would feel cold, so on went the shirts. Ray was used to everyone in his pack train keeping their shirts on all the time. Lillian (up front), heard him say in his droll way "These dudes, one minute I look around and they have next to nothing on, then I look again and they have heavy jackets on."

We were "dudes", a term evenly applied to everyone who books with an outfitter. It just means that clients are most likely city people; they would come with all their new western duds and part of the adventure would be to wear the clothes. This was new to him, he said, looking back and seeing that the dudes had their shirts off. It really made him wonder, but we explained how important it was to be sun-tanned.

Then one day we happened to come upon Ray trudging around the camp site solemnly attending to chores, pant legs rolled up as high as he could get them! Those legs were a sight, white as the snow on the mountains. Was he converted? Not really.

Back to more serious activity, this was the day we would cross our first pass. Soon after we started out that morning we saw a herd of about thirty-five caribou, the biggest herd we had seen.

It took us about three hours to reach the summit. We were at 7,450 feet. Getting up there! Ray had been a professional guide for many years, as well he was a forest ranger and he was full of information. He knew the elevations of all the main sites.

As we rode on toward the pass there was a long solid line of mountains on our right. The trail and the ridge of mountains came closer and closer together. Ray said that unusual range was called "Endless Chain Ridge".

We spent some time just taking in the scenery up in the pass. It was lunch time but we waited until we started descending the other side. We had lunch by a tiny creek, then we were off again, so we could make some miles up the trail toward Poboktan Pass. It was a gorgeous day, perfect for our trek.

Lillian would say every day was an "exciting ride" and we agreed.

Coming down from Maligne Pass we followed a stream that joined Poboktan Creek after about eight miles. Poboktan was flowing south-west to join the Sunwapta River. We turned left and rode upstream on a trail along Poboktan Creek that would take us over Poboktan Pass. We kept going, wanting to camp as far up Poboktan as we could.

Ray knew what distances we covered by the time spent traveling. Over rough ground and climbing the horses would likely make four miles an hour at the most. He had this worked out perfectly, in about three hours we came to a good camp spot that was just a short ride from the Poboktan Pass summit. There was good grass among the willows away from the stream.

We got our tent put up, our spruce bows gathered and our beds made.

Pretty soon everything was in order and another delicious supper before us. Not only steaks, but along the trail Beth had noticed mushrooms, and there were plenty more where we were camped. She knew which ones to pick and we ate an enormous supper of steak and mushrooms, with potatoes, green peas and for dessert, canned peaches. I think we still had our adolescent appetites!

We spent some time cleaning up and doing the dishes. Just like at home, the kitchen is a good place to visit. We learned how to clean up properly camp style. We talked Beth into just sitting on a stump and watching, or going for a stroll.

There were mosquitoes. Actually, they were quite bad, we had to admit. But we had some ways to combat them. One way is to make a smudge by piling some green branches on the fire, and then not moving out of the smoke that makes. Mosquitoes don't like people who smell like smoke. Smelling a little of good wood smoke is better, we thought, than getting eaten. In addition, we had our long sleeved jackets on in the evening, and we had lots and lots of citronella. One other trick, just before we went to bed Ray would take a smoking bit of wood from the fire on a shovel, lift the tent flap and push the shovel in on the ground to smoke there for about half a minute, it didn't take much to deter the little pests, at least for the early part of the night, and for us on the ground in there, nothing to notice of smoke or mosquitoes.

The mosquitoes weren't all bad, lots of them means lots of night hawks, fascinating to watch. Nighthawks don't waste time by pecking at insects one at a time, they gather them in mouthfuls as they fly. It's fascinating on a summer evening to watch the nighthawks as they circle and dive through clouds of mosquitoes. Their dive is arrow fast, producing a totally unique sound, very hard to describe, something like a long "Zing".

We did a bit of exploring, but soon came back to sit and watch the shadows move up the mountain sides east of us, we were already in deep shade from the west.

8

Poboktan Pass & The Brazeau

Next morning we awoke to the breakfast bell and the smell of bacon frying, we were again about to be fortified with good coffee and Ray's light and delicious home-made pancakes, with bacon or just with butter and syrup.

We ate first, then scattered our spruce boughs. We dragged our tent over to the pack boxes and got ourselves organized, leaving Beth to pack the food boxes. She was so organized, actually we three just made it sort of crowded, it was just as well to stay out of the way when she was packing everything in the morning. Clean-up after supper was a little less critical. What we really wanted to do was watch Tom and Ray saddle up. We liked hanging around the horses, there was always more for horse crazy girls to learn. Tom had this for us to think about that day. They were a little late saddling up and this is why. He said that it can happen when the grass is particularly thick and a bit wet from rain, (there had been a shower in the night,) the horses might eat and eat until their bellies puff out. "Watch for that", he said, "sometimes they should be brought in to camp early and should stand for an extra hour before being saddled".

We learned more about saddles. Turning one up-side-down Ray showed us how the padding goes down the two sides, but from front to back down the middle is a big empty groove. This space is then over the horse's backbone, it's important to be sure nothing touches the back bone. The slope of the sides should fit either a rounded belly or a more skinny one. And about the cinch! I always wondered just how tight it should be. "Well" Tom said, "it should be very tight, but you should still, just barely, be able to slide your hand, flat, under the strap. To be sure about the saddle, when you have it cinched, slide your hand down in front of the saddle, down the horse's hide, you shouldn't feel any wrinkled skin, that would mean the saddle is too tight."

We brought our saddle bags, tied them behind our saddles and we were ready for our ride over Poboktan Pass.

"Up and off again for the next exciting ride!", that was Lillian, her enthusiasm still high.

The Trail to Poboktan

Whenever we had thought of passes it was narrow craggy places that we had in mind, but Maligne Pass had not been as we expected, and when Ray said "This is Poboktan Pass" we were surprised again. It was not our idea of a pass at all. We realized then that a pass can be gently sloping upland with rounded summits. Realization! A pass is by definition the easiest route by which you can pass over a mountain range. We were told Poboktan Pass was actually higher than Maligne Pass, though at 7,550 feet only about one hundred feet higher. Ten more trips upstairs!

The curious name, Poboktan, we found comes from the Cree word for owl. No doubt Great Horned Owls were prevalent there as they were quite common. We didn't see any owls, but we did see eagles and hawks.

Poboktan pass. Terry and Jo

A few miles past the summit and we began quite a steep descent into a narrow valley. It was almost like a big canyon, the sides were so steep that when we stopped by the stream for lunch Lillian was the first to comment "We have to look straight up to see blue sky".

We had only made about five miles down from the pass, but mostly we just wanted to get to a lower elevation for lunch.

Our trail followed John-John creek, which empties into the Brazeau system further on. A few more miles and the valley widened to become a lovely montane.

There were so many animals. That day we saw caribou again, and at one point we looked across a valley and saw a huge herd of goats, way too many to count. They were evenly-spaced, all headed in the same direction and spread over the whole valley on the side opposite us, heading toward the Brazeau, just like we were. Unfortunately our little black and white cameras were not up to the job of capturing the off-white goats, nor did they capture the bighorn sheep we saw on the far cliffs. This was the first time for us to see the bighorns. Ray pointed them out, standing like sentinels, high on the ramparts on the other side of the valley. Ray said big sheep and mountain goats are often down in the valley in that area, he said "there are lots of them".

Watching Goats.
Foreground, Ray and Duke, standing at R - Tom

Just at break time we came upon a park warden taking his tea break. There was a young fellow with him. They were the first people we had seen since leaving Maligne lake. Of course we were invited to join them and use their tea fire. John, the young man we were introduced to was the son of the U.S. Ambassador to Canada! His dad had got him a summer job working with a park warden in the Alberta Rockies. There was trail and bridge maintenance, caring for horses and tack, and monitoring wildlife; it was a perfect summer job and it came with a great bonus, the opportunity to learn how to live in the wilderness. The young fellow was having the time of his life; we girls were just a little envious. What a "job", riding horseback in the mountains all summer! They were glad to visit, and so were we. The two rangers got in a little "shop talk".

Lunch with the ranger and John.

On this trip the pace was leisurely. When Ray guided the doctors along the trail they had taken detours from time to time, to check out neighboring valleys and mountain sides; looking for game hangouts as well as sightseeing. Keeping only to the trail, we didn't need to hurry. One day we spotted two eagles, soaring in huge circles riding the air currents over a valley. We just sat in our saddles and watched, spellbound. They scarcely needed to move a feather. It was a sight to remember, the green valley rimmed by forest and snow-covered peaks, a little silvery creek winding along below, quiet broken only by the occasional shuffling and bridle jingle of a restless horse, (what are we stopping here for?), alpine flowers in profusion, and over all the eagles soared, like king and queen of the valley. They were golden eagles, Ray said. What pure joy it would be to float like that over a valley in the summer sun! For eagles though, joy is eating. Ray told us they eat anything, dead or alive, as long as it's protein. We watched them for a long time, but they didn't drop and grab anything. Maybe they weren't hungry after all that day, maybe they *were* just enjoying!

At another stop Ray and Beth pointed out a thin and very high waterfall that we could see across the valley from us.

Everywhere there were flowers growing in profusion on the alpine meadows. There was paint brush, we all knew that one, there was purple saxifrage, mountain avens. Lillian knew the names of most of them. Beth said that on late summer trips she had seen whole meadows purple with mountain heather. Later there would be gooseberry and bunchberry, and lots of bear berries!

Every time we looked across a flower strewn meadow there was something in the back of our minds that we didn't give voice to, didn't have words for, then finally it struck us, there were no weeds! No chickweed, no dandelions! The meadows had a clean look. There in the natural world, untended by us, (or because untended by us) a perfect garden grew.

It's only about twelve miles from Poboktan Pass down along the Brazeau Range to Brazeau Lake. A stream called the North West Brazeau River flows from the west right through Brazeau Lake and out the east end to join the Brazeau River a few miles away on the Jasper Park border. Our trail crossed the river right at the east end of the lake. There was a bridge, it seemed that everyone on that trail used the bridge, there was no fording done as far as we could tell from the river banks. We took the bridge.

We did approach it with some trepidation; would Kitty remember the other bridge and get scared? Or could she now take a bridge in stride?

Everything went fine, and when we were all in a line on the bridge Beth took our picture.

Ray and Duke, pack horses, Dusty,Tom (standing), Terry and Sam, Kitty, Lillian (standing) Jo and Breezy last.

Our plan was to camp by the lake outlet that night, there was a ranger's cabin there (though no ranger) but we set up in the yard. As soon as Ray stopped and we brought the saddle horses together the pack horses came as well to get their saddles off. There were no lead ropes on the pack horses on the trail. They all knew the routine and would stay with the pack train.

We always had eleven horses standing there waiting to get their saddles off. We unsaddled our own, and Beth's as well so she could go and get into her "day box" which was always the first one off the horse.

It was still early afternoon. Beth was getting ready to make a big supper. We helped some but she was so organized we felt a little clumsy. She said "Just go ahead and have a walk; get your knees straightened out".

We went to stroll along a level stretch above the river's edge and found ourselves stepping on wild strawberries. Lillian said "Lets get our cups". They were kept hanging by a thong from our saddle horns. Hers was full first, she was such a fast picker! When Ray saw how many berries we had he quickly produced a batch of his light flaky biscuits. He could do that in about ten minutes, he had can of mix he had made and the oven was already hot.

Beth had got out the ham she bought in Jasper. Supper was ham with sautéed pineapple, buttered baked potatoes and corn, topped off with strawberry shortcake. Who would have thought that trail riders up there in the vast wilderness of the Brazeau would sit down to such a meal.

It had turned out to be a pretty long day after all. Finally, off to bed. What sleeps we had in the mountain air! One night Lillian turned in early and slept for twelve hours.

We were laying over next day at the Brazeau. We spent the day resting, snacking, hiking and enjoying the scenery, the silence, the beautiful spruce forest and high mountains rising in the background. In 1935 there was a landslide there, a huge slab of the mountain slid down right to the edge of the lake, exposing colorful ore deposits. There was no color any more but the vast scrape on the mountain side was impressive.

Brazeau Slide

We hiked around and up near-by hills, not straying too far. Some of the hills rose so smoothly we were tempted to return to childhood and do "roll down the hill". We didn't, the adult in us took over; there were a lot of rocks.

In the afternoon Lillian and Terry decided to try the little river for fish, successfully hooking three nice trout. Beth fried them up for supper.

Lillian hiking

Tom and Ray spent a lot of time that day checking all the horses, especially the pack horses' backs, looking for any pressure spots, and checking all their feet. That's forty-four feet! Traveling over mountain territory there was ample chance for a little stone to get stuck on the underside of a horse's hoof, next to the "frog". It might not cause limping at first, but if not found and taken out there will always be trouble.

Ray's five pack horses were cayuse breed, or at least part cayuse. He said it was pretty hard to find purebreds any more, but his had a lot of cayuse in them nonetheless.

We had thought a cayuse was just any old horse, but it's not so. They were a breed especially sturdy and of even temperament, which made them perfect for pack horses. They had bigger bones and were stronger, able to carry heavy loads all day long. They had wider feet also, which helps on soft ground.

Pack horses in early 1900s really needed to be tough and unflappable. There are lots of stories about the accomplishments of plow horses and cowboy's horses, but not a lot about how the early surveyors and explorers went into the mountains with pack horses. Not only were trails barely negotiable due to bogs and windfall that had to be climbed over, (it often scratched the horses legs), in addition to all that the horses had to carry some of the most outlandish equipment for the surveyors and mountain climbers. They couldn't get skittish just because tripods, telescopes, poles and things that rattled and banged were piled on their backs. Nor could an outfitter's horse object to having a huge rack from a moose or caribou piled onto its back. Many of these stories are found in *Climbs and Explorations in the Canadian Rockies*, **Stutfield and Collie.**

Ray's pack horses had an easier life, the trails were better and they carried nice even loads well tied down and most likely not noisy.

All 5 packhorses ready. LtoR Jo, Tom, Theresa, Lillian, Beth.

After supper on our day off at Brazeau, and after the cribbage game, Beth and Ray were looking for still more entertainment and we challenged them with a few card games from our repertoire.

Tom had disappeared as usual, it was pretty ordinary for him to see some moose and deer on his walk, so common he didn't break his usual silence to mention it. But that night he came back with a story he just had to tell. He had come upon two grizzly bears fighting! He had heard no sound, but when he topped a rise there they were less than a hundred yards away.

He was down-wind from them, so they were unaware of him. Obsessed with their fight they stood tall, growling and swatting at each other with their long claws out; snapping and chewing at each other, they looked dangerous to say the least. Tom didn't watch for too long! We speculated about possible reasons for the fight. Would it be about territory? Fishing rights? A girl grizzly? Maybe all three?

We got ready for bed. The river water was very cold for our baths and the mosquitos were out, we were very quick with our ablutions!

We slept well, confident the grizzlies would keep to themselves.

9

To Nigel Creek

Next morning the breakfast bell woke us at 6am and we scrambled to get ready. We had a long ride ahead of us, all the way to the headwaters of the Brazeau near Nigel Pass, about twenty-five miles from Brazeau Lake where we were camped. We were soon out to the Brazeau River where the trail turned south and followed the river to its rise near Nigel Pass. All the way south we were following part of the eastern boundary of Jasper National Park. From Nigel Creek we would turn east and connect with Cataract Creek and finally trail over Cataract Pass.

It was a beautiful ride all the way up the river valley, on the horizon both to the east and the west are high mountain ranges. Marble Mountain in the west, and in the east, McDonald Mountain and Afternoon Peak are most spectacular. Best of all was that many times that day we saw, right down in the valley, mountain goats and the iconic big horn sheep.

Ray and Beth would stop sometimes and just look, taking it all in. For them it was something more than just a beautiful place, it was like they were part of this natural world. Content and complete just to Be. They had come on this trip, they told us, on their honeymoon. Their love of the wilderness was different than ours. We were just having a great time looking at beautiful scenery. With them it was like they were really where they belonged.

Breezy and I always took some ribbing about being last; we were called "slowpokes", or were told: "Try not to get too far behind, we'd hate to have to come looking for you". It was silly, really, to say we were slow pokes, we moved along just as fast any part of the pack train. The best thing was that we were content, not always pushing around wanting a different place. From our vantage point in the rear we could watch the whole train. There were many streams to ford, some of them a good size and when we were coming to a ford the first ones to cross would turn a right-angle ahead of us and we could watch to see how deep the water was and if the horses were struggling with finding footing.

Because of certain shoreline changes we were to ford the mighty Brazeau three times. Of course it got a lot less "mighty" as we went upstream, but our first ford was right after we turned south.

Quite often in the mountains the streambeds are covered with big round rocks, and it's very difficult for a hoofed animal to find footing. When it's a gravelly and fairly smooth ford it's a joke to cross, but when the river bed is covered with round boulders a horse would most likely rather swim. They don't mind swimming, but mountain streams are inevitably too shallow for swimming, so the horses just have to make the best of it, hoping that all four hooves don't slide at once on the round rocks.

Ray had a word for us before we started across the first ford, "Keep your horse pushing up-stream, against the current, make sure you don't get on the down-stream side of that big rock". Well Kitty didn't see why she should push against the current, so she didn't, (wouldn't), and she drifted, ended up below the rock and she plunged into a hole, into water half-way up the saddle. We always had our feet free of the stirrups when entering water, just in case. Lillian was able to instantly snatch her legs up onto Kitty's neck, holding onto the saddle horn for dear life. Kitty gave a few mighty lunges and was out. Lillian luckily didn't even get wet, but it could have been much worse.

Fording the Brazeau.
Still back in the bush would be Jo and Breezy.

The other two fords were fairly uneventful.

All this time Ray had been trying to worry us about Cataract Pass. Did we think the passes so far had been pretty tame?

"Well" he told us "Cataract will be a different story. Be prepared to get roped over the pass" he said. "We may all have to help the pack horses get over. Two or three of us with a good hold on a long rope, and we'll pull them over".

We weren't sure what to think as we got closer and closer to Cataract.

There is some basis for what Ray said, there have been times when people had to dismount to get over a high place. One instance is recorded in Martin Nordegg's book "*To The Town That Bears Your Name*". That situation though was when the weather was very bad and the wind was blowing a gale. People got off the horses at a pass as much to get out of some of the wind as anything, and they did pull on the horses' lead rope to proceed.

10

Cataract & Sunset

In the afternoon we crossed one Brazeau River feeder coming from the east, Cline Creek, and there was another from the west, Four Point Creek. After that it was not much of a river, we were at its source. The trail continued on straight over a divide and south along Nigel Creek to the N. Saskatchewan River. We would be turning east in the morning. We camped for the night by the Brazeau headwaters, about three hours from Cataract Pass. That pass was going to be a highlight.

In the morning we were pretty excited. From Lillian's diary:

"The scenery all along the trail to Cataract Pass was most beautiful. We climbed higher and higher. Vegetation got thinner and thinner until there wasn't any. No trees, no grass, iron horse shoes clanking on bare rock. We reached the summit before noon. We had arrived! We were above the tree-line to where there was only snow, rock and water, but there were the most beautiful little flowers growing out of very thin soil! There were columbines, yellow, white, pink and red, also very beautiful forget-me-nots".

It's an unexpected delight for the inexperienced mountain trekker to find that where the climate is too severe for trees to grow wildflowers bloom, the early ones as soon as the snow melts, later varieties in their time.

It was a steep rocky climb, but no, as it turned out we didn't have to dismount! The horses managed.

It was perfectly still and silent, a world of blinding white snow, blue meltwater, and solid rock, all under a brilliant blue sky. Very soon the short mountain summer would be over and there would be only blue and white. On a high cliff in the distance we saw mountain goats keeping watch.

We were at 8,200 feet, the highest point we would reach. We were about one hundred miles from Jasper.

Summit Lake, Cataract Pass

Up and Over Cataract

Jo, (Sinatra jacket,) and Lillian

Breezy and Jo take a break

We looked around for a while at the top, nothing changed! The horses had a breather, then it was on and over. I think the horses were uneasy up there, there was no grass!

One more much appreciated feature of this pass, and all passes and high places, there were no flies up there! Black flies are often quite bothersome in the wilderness.

We followed Cataract Creek all the way down from the pass. As we got to a lower level we stopped for lunch, then we were in forest again on a one way trail. There was lots of activity in the bush, we didn't see any big animals there, mostly they are down on the montanes, but squirrels and little animals and birds chattered and busied themselves constantly. We saw porcupine twice, one appeared ambling along the trail in front of us. Ray didn't want to excite him and we all slowed down as much as we could, making all the horses behind Duke restless, wondering just what was going on. Finally porky got to his turn-off and disappeared into the bush.

From Lillian's diary:

"When we got down lower in the valley, we set up camp for the night. It rained soon after we got set up. Except for one shower during the night, this was the first rain we had and we'd been on the trail for a week! We've had the most beautiful weather all the time for our trip. It was still dripping a bit when we went to bed. We went to sleep listening to the patter of drops on the tent roof. After seven nights out our spruce bough beds are feeling softer!"

11

Pinto Lake

Next day we stopped for an early lunch break where Cataract Creek empties into the Cline River. The Cline Trail would be our route east, but not until later. There was a little wooden sign "Pinto Lake" nailed to a tree and pointing south. Pinto was to be our next camp site and from there we would access Sunset Pass. It was only another few miles to the lake, following upstream along the Cline. Close to the lake we crossed Huntington Creek flowing into the Cline from the east.

We set up camp near the lake at the north end. There couldn't have been a more beautiful spot. We had seen nothing but beautiful spots, but Pinto Lake is surely one of the most exquisite mountain lakes. The reflections of forest and mountain are extraordinary as always but the glacial run-off in tiny Pinto Lake contains more varied mineral silts and in higher concentrations than usual. These silts impart more and different variations of greens and blues in striking combinations in the reflections on the water. Patches of color could have led early travelers to the name "Pinto". There is a second story, one that says a surveyor's troublesome packhorse named Pinto made his escape there.

Sunset is more than 1000 feet lower than Cataract, but isolated and very much more treacherous and steep the first part of the way up, especially from the south. The way up from the south is a bad place for horses, it's mostly rocky steps. Horses have come to a bad end negotiating the south trail up Sunset Pass.

There is easier access from the north end of Pinto Lake. After we were set up we girls and Tom rode back about a mile north up the trail to Huntington Creek, followed it a short distance east, turned left and followed a rough trail south, making a loop. Continuing south through lodgepole pine east of the lake we began the climb up Sunset. We soon left the horses tied to some deadfall and hiked the rest of the way. It was a rough, steep climb, but the reward was sensational. High up on Sunset is a plateau, "Sunset Meadows".

What a view! Far below to the north we could see the vast panorama of the North Saskatchewan River valley. Beyond that a view of the mountains on the continental divide, their peaks covered with glaciers. Below us on our right was a view of Pinto Lake. It was truly breathtaking. We spent a long time just looking, it was late afternoon when we headed back to camp, and supper.

Lillian – View of Pinto Lake and the North Saskatchewan River valley.

We were "laying over" at Pinto. Next morning after breakfast it was time for more hiking and sightseeing.

A small mountain rises up beside Pinto Lake. Climbing to the top of some big hill usually reveals a bigger hill behind, a summit not reachable. This little mountain looked to be by itself, quite easy to climb, nothing dangerous or very difficult, it looked just right..

In the early afternoon Lillian, Terry and I walked along the lakeshore until we came to a trail going up the mountain. Tom came with us. We all started to climb up, but after about half an hour Lillian and Terry announced they were going back. I had no intention of turning back. It was an easy climb. Looking back at the lake from about half way up was proof that I was getting somewhere, the lake looked about half as big.

Tom had not turned back, I assumed that, like me, he just wanted to get to the top. He didn't say anything, he just kept climbing up. Thinking about that later on I realized that it was very likely foolhardy of me to keep going on alone. There was ample chance for at least a sprained ankle.

It was not all a walk, we encountered a very steep crevasse, littered with little boulders and scree, we were going to have to traverse that if we kept going. It was a scramble on all fours, but only for about 100 yards. I had on good heavy boots. More than once, as Lillian said, we thankfully had got ourselves the right thing, hob-nailed boots. After about four hours we came to the top, the actual summit. Although there were snow-clad mountains surrounding, they were not part of this mountain. It was a summit! There was a sheer drop-off in the direction of our camp. I didn't walk to the edge. I got that tingly feeling in the back of my legs as soon as we got up there. I thought that whoever had built the cairn had set it way to close to the edge. I sat on it with my back to the drop-off for the picture Tom took for me. We could see the tiny figures busy at our camp far below. They were watching, they said later that we looked like "little sticks."

Perched on the cairn, gingerly

Beth with our supper

Terry naps on the boxes

Ray's exercise equipment

During our climb, Beth, one not given to idle pursuits, had made raisin pie and then with time left over she coaxed a big trout from the lake for our supper.

Like good big sisters Terry and Lilliian had done laundry. A little fawn hung around the camp and Terry said it tried to take our pyjamas!

Beth wouldn't take credit for catching the fish, she said the lake was full of them and they practically fought over her hook. We had a feast! The trout was delicious, the flesh a little pink, it was almost like eating salmon. In fact we joked that it was local salmon. At dinner that night:

A la carte, grilled Pinto Lake salmon (Ray said it was cutthroat trout.)

> honey mustard sauce
> Rice and green peas.
> Mixed veggies.
> Raisin pie.

After cleanup we wandered down to the lake to watch shore birds and stare at the schools of minnows in the crystal clear water. That afternoon Ray had put up a swing. For exercise he said, so later we obliged, pushing each other like kids. Really though we'd had a long day and we were ready for campfire and bed.

Tom got back from his evening walk, quiet as usual. I sometimes thought maybe he talked only to the horses. He liked to go for a walk alone and he always saw some animal. In the dusk of the late evening he would come to the campfire, sit on a log, or the ground, and roll a smoke. It was his late-evening ritual, the practiced moves automatic: From a side pocket the green package of Turret tobacco. From inside the package the tiny red pack of Chanticleer cigarette papers, all packed in so that when you pull one out its fold brings out the next one, just like Kleenex. Left thumb and finger hold the little paper, gummed edge on the far side, a big pinch of tobacco carefully placed on the paper, two forefingers even out and pack, two thumbs roll the bottom edge over the tobacco, back and forth twice, roll almost to the top edge, lick, stick, light with a burning twig from the fire.

Whiffs of clean tobacco smoke drift in the air. It's very peaceful and quiet. Pretty soon we head for our tent and bed.

12

The Cline River Trail

Lillian and Kitty. Peak with the cairn behind.
Four miles from Sunset

Next morning it was time to fold up our Pinto Lake camp and move on. After our usual great breakfast we packed up and got an early start. The Cline River has its origin south of Pinto Lake, it flows into the lake and shows up again coming out of the north end of the lake. We were to follow the Cline from Pinto Lake all the way to the North Saskatchewan River, about thirty miles We were on the north shore of the Cline as we left our campsite, we crossed Huntington Creek and then Cataract

Creek, passing the Pinto Lake sign and on we went down the Cline River Trail. There were many small creeks to ford.

Ray called the Cline River the Whitegoat. There was a basis for that, it was called the Whitegoat earlier by explorers with the Palliser expedition. They actually used the native word for whitegoat, calling it the Waputekh River. Cline was the name of one of the earlier explorers and his name got assigned to the river. It has happened many times that more than one name has got assigned to a geographical feature. In situations like that the names must be sifted out at some point and a government decision made as to what is to be the legal name. This one came up "Cline River".

The whole area from the Cline sloping north to the front range of the mountains is called the Whitegoat. It's a vast wilderness area with the most spectacular views up to a backdrop of high glacier-covered mountains. We rode through clean stands of lodgepole pine and sometimes down lower along meadows with patches of poplar and birch. We saw so many birds! Ray and Beth named for us the ones we didn't know such as yellow warblers, (we called them canaries, wrong!). We saw pine siskins, finch, hummingbirds, cedar waxwing, bluebirds. It was like a sanctuary. Overhead eagles soared; bald eagles they were, this time.

Terry was an accomplished pianist and soloist. Something about the forest made her feel like singing and she delighted us with beautiful solos. On the "charts" were the hits of Nelson Eddy and Jeanette MacDonald. Terry knew all their songs, and she knew all the words. We heard *Without A Song, Only A Rose, I married An Angel, I'll Be Loving You, Indian Love Call*. The forest was "alive with the sound of music". Maybe it was the cathedral-like atmosphere that a forest lends that brought forth music. I had to wonder just how many pairs of bright little eyes stared out from their cover, transfixed by the strange sights and sounds.

After about twelve miles we came to McDonald Creek, one of two good-sized creeks that feed the Cline, the other is Coral Creek. Each of these creeks drain huge areas from the north and are fed by literally dozens and dozens of little streams so they are big and fast when they enter the Cline. Fording the McDonald it was a bit of a struggle for the horses to keep their footing but as usual they managed.

After we got across the creek we took a break, this time for coffee along with our sandwiches. Several of the horses got impatient and tried to roll with the saddles and pack-boxes on, which was curious as they had just come off a day's rest at Pinto.

McDonald Creek lunch

On the Cline River Trail

Riding on after lunch our trail was often high above the river. It was such a beautiful ride. South of the Cline it's lower and wet, with swamp spruce and boggy places. That's why Ray chose the north side trail. At one point we looked across to the south and saw moose down there.

Nearly every day on this entire trip there were times when we topped a rise, or emerged from a forest, that within sight was such overwhelming space and distance as to make us feel tiny and insignificant, and that surely our progress would count only as inches.

All along the montane it was the perfect place for wildlife. We saw lots of goats, deer with twin fawns, one with one, and some caribou.

Continuing along the Cline there were numerous little creeks to cross, plus Coral Creek, big and fast as the McDonald. After many miles we said goodbye to the Cline, crossed a bridge at White Goat Crossing and rode east toward the North Saskatchewan River and the Kootenay Plains. It was a long ride that day.

The first thing we saw on the Plains was a herd of wild horses. They had been watching us, when they had seen enough the stallion gave us a disdainful toss of his head and they all loped smoothly away, long manes and tails streaming in the breeze.

Right after seeing the horses we set up camp and soon sat down to a good supper. A beautiful little hummingbird hovered around while we were eating supper. Again there were lots of wild strawberries! They were everywhere, ripe and delicious.

In the mountains dusk comes very quickly when the afternoon sun slides behind a mountain. This was the first time on the trip that there was a little more sky, and even a little sunset. We didn't stay up long though, we "hit the sack". Next day we were to see a lot more of the Plains.

When we rode onto the Kootenay Plains that day we were entering a very special place, one that for hundreds of years has been like an oasis on the eastern slope of the Rockies. Due to some not totally understood variation in mountain landscape, or in the prevailing winds the climate and vegetation of the plains is found nowhere else. The ten mile wide area of prairie wool grasslands interspersed with patches of willow stretched for forty miles, along both sides of the N. Saskatchewan River. The grass is particularly nourishing and has afforded year-round grazing for thousands of hoofed game animals.

The Kootenay Plains have been home and sustenance for native people for many generations. The Kootenay from southern British Columbia came there with furs to trade. To the Stoney and then the Cree it was a land of plenty, providing for their every physical need, and as well it was a place of special spiritual significance for burial grounds and sundance sites. We saw two of the large tipis that were used for sundance.

13
Across The Kootenays

We were feeling a bit giddy and somewhat nostalgic at the same time as we started across the Kootenay Plains next morning. This would be our last long day in the saddle, our last long day to soak up the wilderness.

We would have many wonderful memories, of magnificent scenery, of vast space, of life on a wilderness trail, of the horses, and of wild strawberries! There they were again, on our last day, in profusion. They were so thick we couldn't pass them by; we got off and ate as fast as we could, galloped to catch up, got off and ate more, then back in the saddle, hands all stained with strawberry juice.

We saw more wild horses, a deer, a squirrel and even a grasshopper! (That last one noticed by Lillian, who noticed *everything*.)

About mid-day the horses pricked up their ears, then we heard it as well, the grinding sound of a car motor in low gear. A motor! Up Here!

"Oh-Oh!" – This from Ray

Coming toward us was an old Model A Ford, and in it four men who were in very high spirits, having come over Windy Point, as they were soon to tell us. They greeted us,

"Hey! What's going on here?"

"We've come from Jasper."

They kept their motor running and talked very loud, sometimes more than one at a time. There was lots of laughter as they told their story.

"We're The Trail Blazers. You must have heard about us, we're from Rocky, (Rocky Mountain House) We've come over Windy Point! Lots of cars are coming over now. They winch over Windy Point! (more laughter) Winch or block and tackle. This little baby (the Model A) we could just about carry her over!" (More laughter) We're Pioneers!"

"Where did you say you came from?"

"We've come from Jasper."

"From Jasper on horses. Well how about that. Well, just wait, next time you'll be able to whiz through here in a car, in a couple of hours. There'll be a road through here, you'll see; the government will have to pay attention now. We've proved it can happen."

We just sat our horses and they talked.

"We're working to get a highway up here, makes a lot of sense. Right through to the Banff Jasper highway. We've proved it's possible. We're pioneers!"

"This country's going to open up, you'll see. We even hear talk about a dam up here. Now wouldn't that be something? Well we're gonna make a few more miles".

They got in the Model A and moved on. They were following a trail they had marked out before, every little way they would stop and move a rock out of the way to make their little trail where they wanted it.

We were subdued as we rode along toward Windy Point. We didn't say anything for a long time, didn't try to analyze some vague feeling that we were, somehow, diminished. It didn't help that we met more people, all day we met car loads of people who were following the trail of the Model A.

We had to eat supper close to other people who had come by car.

We stopped at the Windy Point outlook to hold our hats on and look west at the headwaters of the North Saskatchewan river, "braided" along the bottom of a wide deep valley that stretched as far as we could see. We rode on to the Bighorn River. We were only eight miles from Nordegg.

On Windy Point we have to hold onto our hats.

We stopped and made our supper; again there were other people in the camp spot who had come by car from Rocky.

Back to civilization!

We continued on after supper, thinking about what it would be like to be home. Hot bath water did come to mind, a real bed, our *Jobs*. Theresa was off school for the whole summer.

We stopped for a drink at Shunda Creek. There was a forestry road, and a bridge over the creek.

Back to Civilization - Drinking From Shunda Creek.

It was getting dark when we finally trailed into the Nordegg Forestry station grounds.

We girls said goodbye to Sam and Breezy and Kitty. We gave them a slap and told them "Good boy, Good girl". They were non-committal, wanting only to be unsaddled and turned out to home grass. They had earned their time off, bringing us safely over many steep and rocky miles.

We put up our tents for our last night out. The ranger's big cat got into the tent with us hoping for a cozy bed.

Next morning, July 15, we packed our few things and looked around the little town of Nordegg. We all had dinner in a restaurant. Then it was time to say goodbye to Beth and Ray and to Tom. They came to the railroad station with us and saw us off on the Canadian National Railway train to Rocky Mountain House.

That train ride was the final chapter in our adventure. Although it was only about sixty miles to Rocky Mountain House, it took us about four hours to get there. The train was a "mixed", it traveled very slowly, there were places to stop, so we stopped at each place. There was Horburg, Saunders Creek, Alexo, Ferrier, all very small villages.

As the train rattled along we began to daydream. Maybe we *could* have our own horses some day, after all. It would not be impossible. There were places near town where horses could be boarded.

Some day we could ride again.

Epilogue

Many thanks to Lillian for making this work possible. She's the one who has kept the memories alive, written all the notes and saved all the photos. She is the one who has made it possible for us to re-capture these memories. What a ride! We had the time of our young lives.

We intended that our ride to remember be more than a trip committed only to memory. When the trip was over and we were home again we immediately began planning how we would "write it up". At the very least we would produce something for the local paper, for our families, or for other trail riders.

Life happened. Later that year we girls all married. Time passed quickly, families grew, careers demanded. Decades passed. People died, among them our friend Theresa, the Mustards and Tom. We got old. Now it's 2011 and our story is history; we write of a time when horses were *de rigueur* on the trails, when we slept on spruce boughs and drank from the streams. Alpine meadows had no weeds. There was no chopper, no cell phone, no GPS, no plastic wrap.
There are two of us now, we could still ride, but the trail would need to be much shorter.

Theresa Dickinson Glover
1924 - 1971

Appendix

Packing the pack horse, by Mary Luger
First a halter with a lead rope or halter shank is put on the pack horse's head. The horse is tied to a tree or to a rail for saddling and packing. The horse is brushed to remove any dirt from his back, then a thick blanket and/or pack pad is placed on the horse's back. The pack saddle with a front and back cinch is placed on the horse. The two cinches are tightened using the leather straps or latigos, the front cinch is placed just behind the horses front legs and the back cinch near the back of the belly. A tie between the two cinches keeps the back cinch from moving too far back. A pack saddle may also have a breast plate on the front to go around the horses chest to keep the saddle from moving back going up a hill. It may also have back breeching which is a strap like a breast plate that goes around the horses rump to keep the saddle from moving ahead when going down hill.

Most commonly used in Alberta was a carved wooden pack saddle known as a sawbuck saddle. A lightweight 3/8" rope about 30' long called the basket rope attaches to the front forks of the pack saddle allowing half of the rope to be used on each side of the horse to support a pack box. These ropes were strung between the front and back forks of the saddle looping around the center of the pack box and then under it to support the box and tied in center of each pack box to finish the basket hitch. Bulky items like bed rolls, tents etc. were generally put in a tied bundle and placed on top of the pack boxes for the top pack. The two free ends of the basket rope, one with a loop in it, are brought together over the top pack and snugged down tight and tied. A pack cover tarp generally 5' x 7' in size was placed over the top pack to keep the pack together and dry during a rain storm.

The lash cinch is about 36" long with a ring on one end with a 3/4" rope about 30' long tied to it and a hook on the other end. The hook was generally of carved wood with a bolt through it for strength. The lash rope is used to tie the diamond hitch on top of the pack tarp. To tie a standard diamond hitch the rope is laid over the top of the pack about center of the horse from back to front with most of the rope out behind the horse. The lash cinch is placed over the top of the pack and brought under the horse's belly. The rope is hooked on the cinch hook on the left or near-side and the cinch is drawn up tight on the horse's belly with the rope sliding through the hook. The lash cinch is positioned on top of or just back of the pack saddle's front cinch. The lash rope is then wrapped twice under the tight rope passing over the top pack from side to side forming a V to the front side of the rope. The tail end of the rope is pulled through the V giving enough slack in the rope to make a wrap on each side around the undersides of the two pack boxes, first on the off-side and then on the near-side. One person pulls the slack from the rope around the pack box on the off-side while the second person tightens the rope on the box on the near-side. The tail end of the rope is then tugged tight from the back of the horse and this forms the diamond shape of the hitch on the top center of the pack tarp. The end of the rope is tied off in a loop and secured with a couple of half hitches that will be easy to remove. The remainder of the rope is tied in a few chain loops and secured on the pack so it will not drag or catch.

The lead rope on the halter of the pack horse is either held by a rider on horseback or tied to another pack horse's tail to form a string of pack horses. A nose net or nose basket is placed over the horse's nose so that he will not stop to eat while on the move, but can drink water through the mesh.

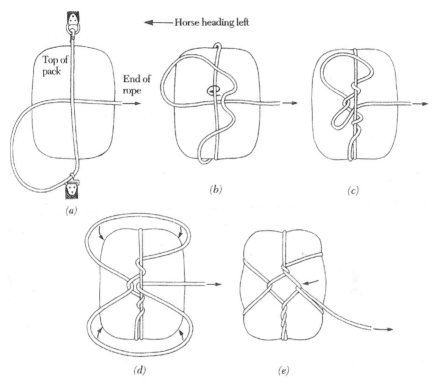

Top of pack

End of rope

Horse heading left

(a)

(b)

(c)

(d)

(e)

Diamond hitch diagram

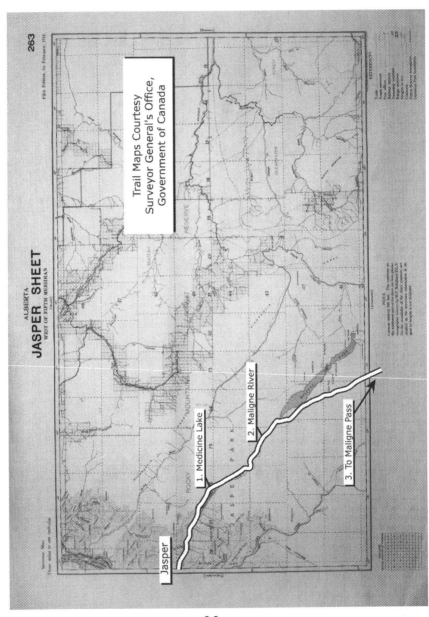

Map

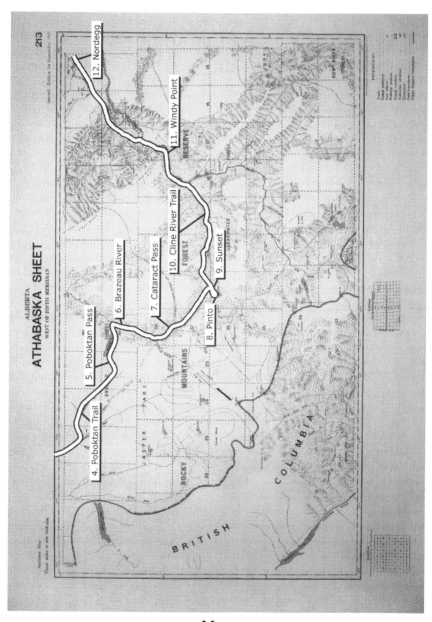

Map

Acknowledgements

For reminders that trigger a memory, for stories, maps and statistics, for corroboration and information and technical help I am indebted to:

Ameera Shivi, TransAlta
Betty Mustard Dionne
Connie Jo Smith
Garry Fix
Horse Shoe In My Hip Pocket - Bob Kjos
Jacqueline Price
Jean-Marie Mason, Rocky Mountain House Museum
Jim Belliveau – *Belliveau Art & Design*
Katherine Boychuk
Jonathan Meakin, Alberta Foundation for the Arts
Ken Janigo, Alberta Sustainable Resources
Lillian and Sam Glover
Lindsay Moir, Glenbow Museum
Meghan Power, Jasper Museum
Nigel Douglas, Alberta Wilderness Society
Paul Peyto
People and Peaks of Wilmore Wilderness - Susan Feddema-Leonard
Rock Abraham
Roger Rinker
Ronald Kelland, Historical Places Research Officer
Tom and Shawn Vinson
Yvette Vinson

RESOURCES

Black Bond Books
Landsdowne Centre
214-5300 No. 3 Road
Richmond B.C. (604)274-7203
bbbconnie@hotmail.com

jacquelineprice4@hotmail.com
jacquelineprice.com or
jpillustration.ca
"THE ART OF AN
ILLUSTRATOR
IS TO CREATE FOR YOU"

Old Entrance B 'n B Cabins
26118 Old Entrance Road
PO Box 6054, Hinton AB
T7V 1X4
Phone: 780-865-4760
Website: http://www.oldentrance.
ab.ca

Horseback Adventures Ltd.
Tom & Shawn Vinson
P.O. Box 73, Brule, AB
Canada T0E 0C0

Timberline Tours Ltd.
Paul Peyto
Box 14, Lake Louise AB
T0L 1E0

Willmore Wilderness Foundation
1.780.827.2696 or 1.866.
WILMORE
A Registered Charitable
Organization #89655 0308
RR0001
4600 Pine Plaza | Box 93 Grande
Cache, Alberta |780-827-2696
http://www.WillmoreWilderness.
com | http://www.PeopleandPeaks.
com

ART & DESIGN
bellart@telusplanet.net